Copyright © 201‍

All rights reserved. No part of this publication may be reproduced, distributed, or transmitted in any form or by any means, including photocopying, recording, or other electronic or mechanical methods, without the prior written permission of the publisher, except in the case of brief quotations embodied in critical reviews and certain other noncommercial uses permitted by copyright law.

First Edition

Unless otherwise noted, all Scripture quotations are taken from the Holy Bible, New Living Translation (NLT) © 1996, 2004, 2007. Used by permission of Tyndale House Publishers, Inc., Wheaton, Illinois 60189. All rights reserved.

Scripture quotations marked NIV are taken from the Holy Bible, New International Version, NIV .© 1973, 1978, 1984, 2011 by Biblica, Inc. Used by permission of Zondervan. All rights reserved worldwide. www.zondervan.com

Scripture quotations marked NKJV are from THE NEW KING JAMES VERSION.© 1982 by Thomas Nelson, Inc. Used by permission. All rights reserved.

Written by: Tiffany Langford

Cover Design by: Tiffany Langford & Rachel Rhule (Rachel.rhule@gmail.com)

Connect with Us

Website

waitingforyourboaz.com

Facebook

facebook.com/waitingforyourboaz

Twitter

twitter.com/waiting_on_boaz

Pinterest

pinterest.com/waitingforyourboaz

Instagram

instagram.com/waitingforyourboaz

Other Books by Tiffany

31 Days of Prayer for Your Future Husband

Becoming a Proverbs 31 Woman

I Love You More Than the Moon and Stars

Letters to My Future Husband

31 Days of Prayer for My Husband

Table of Contents

FORWARD	7
PRAYER FOR THE READER	15
DAY 1: SHE PURSUES JESUS	18
DAY 2: SHE EMBODIES HUMILITY	24
DAY 3: SHE CHERISHES WISDOM	30
DAY 4: SHE EXEMPLIFIES GENEROSITY	35
DAY 5: SHE FOLLOWS PEACE	41
DAY 6: SHE HAS A SERVANT'S	47
HEART	47
DAY 7: SHE EMBODIES STRENGTH	52
DAY 8: SHE WALKS IN EXCELLENCE	57
DAY 9: SHE IS VIRTUOUS	62
DAY 10: SHE MODELS GRACE	67

DAY 11: SHE IS A HELPMATE	**72**
DAY 12: SHE EMBRACES INTIMACY	**77**
DAY 13: SHE EXEMPLIFIES INNER BEAUTY	**82**
DAY 14: SHE ABIDES IN GRATITUDE	**87**
DAY 15: SHE CHERISHES JOY	**92**
DAY 16: SHE WALKS IN LOVE	**97**
DAY 17: SHE FOLLOWS MERCY	**102**
DAY 18: SHE EMBRACES COMPASSION	**107**
DAY 19: SHE IS FAITHFUL	**112**
DAY 20: SHE WALKS IN FORGIVENESS	**117**
DAY 21: SHE DWELLS IN INTEGRITY	**122**
DAY 22: SHE HAS UNSHAKABLE FAITH	**127**
DAY 23: SHE ENCOURAGES	**132**
DAY 24: SHE CLEARLY COMMUNICATES	**137**
DAY 25: SHE WALKS IN PURITY	**142**

DAY 26: SHE EMBRACES OBEDIENCE	**147**
DAY 27: SHE IS A VISIONARY	**152**
DAY 28: SHE IS RESOLUTE	**156**
DAY 29: SHE WALKS IN CONFIDENCE	**161**
DAY 30: SHE IS AFTER GOD'S OWN HEART	**166**
ABOUT THE AUTHOR	**172**

Forward

"Father,

You know this road isn't easy for me. You know my heart's desire; to love and be loved. You see where I've come from in life, and you see where I'm going but in this moment, waiting on you is just so difficult.

I'm surrounded by a culture pushing me into ideas and ways that I know do not align with your will for me. My heart tries to pursue, yet you tell me to wait. I know that I am your cherished daughter and I know the plans you have for me are great but I pray right now, in this moment, you fill me with your peace.

Help me to become fully satisfied in you, before you bring my Boaz to me. Help me to trust the process of becoming the woman you desire for me to be. You see my heart's full potential. You know that when I love, I love deeply and when I fall, I fall hard. Father save my heart for the man you have set aside for me. Prepare me to be the kind of wife he needs me to be. But more than anything, I long to be a wife after your own heart.

I choose to fully chase after you, God. When you bring along the man I am meant to marry I will not stop chasing you. We will chase after you together. We will be each other's helpmate. We will love each other purely and deeply, but we will love you the most. We will constantly strive to keep you at the center of our lives and marriage, for I know you are the glue that will hold us together. When my Boaz comes along I will not forget my first love.

I will not forget the one who loved me first, and loved me enough to give me a godly man who will love, cherish, and treasure the woman that I am. While I am here waiting on you, I will choose to serve. I will choose to chase after your heart. I will choose to embrace all that you have called me to be. Wherever you go, I'll go. Wherever you stay, I will stay. I will leave the world behind to chase after the God of my heart. I will trust in you, even when the road seems hard and I feel like I can't take another step.

I will let you mold me into the wife you have called me to be. I will love, cherish, honor, and treasure my future spouse. I will rely on the covenant of marriage and your strength to bring me through when my emotions attempt to lead me astray. I thank you for all that you are and all that you are preparing me to be. I thank you that I can trust you with every single detail of my life, because I know everything that matters to me matters to you.
I know that in your perfect timing, when you see fit, you will bring us both together to love and serve you. Thank you for loving me.

Love,

You're treasured daughter

* * * * * *

Tears were streaming down my cheeks as I prayed this prayer. As a young woman, I found myself longing for a love story that only God could give me, but little did I know the pruning process that God was getting ready to take me through in order to fulfill His purpose in my life not only from a perspective of marriage, but from every single aspect of my life.

I gave my heart to God at a young age. My pursuit of God far outweighed anything this world could give me. As I began to mature in Christ I came to the understanding that God had a love story for me and longed to give me the desires of my heart, but little did I understand that kind of responsibility also called me to test my own heart, allow God to rid me of myself, and to leave some things behind that were holding me back. Instead of focusing so much on finding the right person, God wanted me to focus my energy into *becoming* the right kind of person, the kind of wife my future husband needed.

As time continued on, throughout this process I often found myself regretting that decision to ask God to prepare me. I would pray, "God, prepare me for my calling. God, prepare me to do the work you have for me. God, prepare me for my future husband and our marriage," but when the *preparation* had begun, I became very aware of my own shortcomings and found myself feeling more frustrated, impatient, disappointed in myself than I had ever felt in my entire life.

God began revealing things to me that I had never before realized and places where I needed to grow and mature. There were things I couldn't take into the marriage He had for me, things that had the capability of ruining my life and future marriage before it had even begun. One thing God revealed to me during all of this was that my desire often inclined more toward marriage and finding someone rather than resting in my first love and building my relationship with *Him*, first and foremost. It was a harsh reality when God began testing and trying my heart, but just as I had asked him to do, He knit-picked me in every possible way and today I can honestly say that I'm thankful He did. Still yet, God is pruning me and shaping me into a wife after His own heart.

God is still preparing me to become a godly wife. He is still working on my heart daily to thrive as the woman He has called me to be. Just because I said, "I do," doesn't mean I've obtained perfection. Many days I fall short, and I will be in the process of becoming a godly wife until the day I pass from this earth, and so will you. We all mess up daily and need God's grace daily. We are all a work in progress, and as we walk our own unique destiny road, God often takes us through some hard places, where loneliness and difficulty may engulf your heart.

But everything you are going through right now is preparing you for your future. You are not walking this road alone. God has an incredible plan for your life that far outweighs any present circumstance you may be facing today. But right now in this season, I encourage you to wait. I encourage you to serve the Lord and love Him with all of your heart. I encourage you to learn to love others and serve those around you. I encourage you to cling so tightly to your Savior that you have no room to let anything that is not of Him or from Him into your heart. In doing this, you will discover what it means to become a spotless bride after God's own heart as you wait on the man He has for you.

During this process you will learn to love yourself so much that you could not accept anything less than the best He has for you. When you fall in love with God and begin to mirror His image, He will cause your desires to align with His as He prepares you for your Boaz. If you are already married and long to become more like Him, this journey is for you too. This invitation stands for both the single and married alike, to chase after Christ and allow Him to shape you into the kind of wife and mother He has called you to be.

And the marriage God has for you is definitely something worth praying, preparing, and waiting for.

Prayer for The Reader

Before we begin, I want to say a prayer over you that God would open your heart to receive whatever He has for you in this season. As you begin this devotional, I pray your heart is blessed and your life is changed. As you prepare yourself for the marriage God has for you, I want to encourage you above all else to fall in love with Him and discover the beautiful romance of what it means to dance with Jesus.

Heavenly Father,

I thank you for the person who is reading this. I thank you that she has made the decision to pray for her future husband and to set aside this time in preparation to become the wife her future husband needs. I pray that you would do an enormous thing in her heart and life as she walks this journey with you. Quicken her heart to be still and listen to the Holy Spirit's promptings. Prepare her to be the wife that you have called her to be and I pray she will fall more in love with you every single day. Father, let her know just how crazy you are about her and that you are head over heels in love with her. Show her that she is your treasure, and that you delight in your cherished one.

Open her heart to receive all that you have for her and give her direction to stay on this path you have called her to walk. Hold her hand when she gets weary, and encourage her spirit when she feels as though she cannot take another step. Show her that you will carry her throughout all the days of her life and that you have good things in store for her future.

I speak blessings over her right now. I pray that all the beautiful things you have in store for her will come in Your perfect timing and not one minute sooner. Manifest yourself in a mighty way in her life so that all who see her will know that You are the one who has brought her from the dust and called her to a life of purpose. I thank you Lord for your compassion and covering over her.

In Jesus name,

Amen

Day 1: She Pursues Jesus

Daily Devotion

"Blessed are those who keep His testimonies, who seek Him with their whole heart! They also do no iniquity; they walk in His ways."
Psalm 119:2-3

Everyone has their mind made up about marriage in one way or another. For some, the idea of marriage may seem repulsive. For others, it has become their main pursuit in life. Maybe you were the little girl who played "wedding" with your favorite dolls and dreamed of the day you would meet your prince charming. Or perhaps you were the little girl who watched your parent's marriage fall apart at the seams and swore to yourself that you would never allow your heart to experience that same devastating pain.

While I can't take that pain from you, I just happen to know the One who can, and I believe it is not by chance that this book is in your hands right in this moment. You still have some desire, maybe tucked down very deeply, for a union that only God himself can fabricate. But the first thing I want you to know is this; you do not have to go out and find your happily ever after. The most perfect Prince is standing right in front of you waiting for you to place your hand in His and dance.

His name is Jesus and He loves you with an everlasting love, the kind that puts the love of a thousand lovers to shame. He has the power to take everything wrong in your life and turn it into something beautiful and powerful. You don't need a man to complete you, contrary to popular belief. You are not defined by a romantic relationship and do not require one to be whole. You are complete just as you are, and Jesus is the only one who can satisfy the deepest longings of your heart.

I thought the day I married my sweetheart everything that was wrong in my life would suddenly be made right. But I was, and still am, an imperfect woman married to a wonderful, yet imperfect man in a messy, imperfect world. It didn't take me long to discover that the only one who could truly satisfy my heart was, in fact, the One who created it. With that being said, it is okay to long for and dream of your marriage. It's *essential* to prepare for it as you pray for your future husband and yourself, and wait for the one who is doing the same. But keep in mind there is only one who can fill your heart to the brim. Besides, your future husband shouldn't have to bear the overwhelming burden of your eternal contentment and satisfaction. If you look to mere men to find what only God can provide, you will only find yourself utterly disappointed.

    So consider this your invitation, to begin chasing wildly after the one who spoke life into the depths of your beautiful spirit and loves you perfectly. Consider yourself challenged, to become a woman who is in full pursuit of Abba. Above all else, strive to become a woman after His own heart because the one thing I can assure you of is this; that God-shaped hole inside of your heart will remain there until the day you say, "I do" to Jesus.

Daily Prayer

Heavenly Father,

I thank you for what you have already done in my life and what you are going to do. On this road of preparation to becoming all that you have called me to be, I pray that you would help me to keep my priorities straight and to fix my focus fully on you. I pray that I would never lose sight, but that I would continue to chase hard after you all the days of my life, before and after you have blessed me with the man you have set aside for me.

I pray that nothing would come between us and that we would always keep you at the center of our marriage. I am so in love with you Jesus, and I pray that my love for you would continue to abound more and more, as you continue to reveal your infinite love to me daily. Thank you for being so good to me. Thank you for preparing and molding me into a woman who pursues you wholeheartedly in spirit and in truth. I thank you for saving me for the man you have called me to marry in your perfect timing.

In Jesus name,
Amen

Daily Journal

_____

_____

_____

_____

_____

_____

_____

_____

Scriptures to meditate on:

Psalm 119:2-3
Philippians 3:10-11
James 4:8

Day 2: She Embodies Humility

Daily Devotion

"But the fruit of the Spirit is love, joy, peace, patience, kindness, goodness, faithfulness, gentleness, self-control; against such things is no law."
Galatians 5:22-23

I just couldn't seem to choke the words out, those two humbling yet powerful words that we all know too well, "I'm sorry." I looked at my husband sitting beside me and realized that my words, spoken out of frustration and anger, had deeply wounded him. My heart was crying out to embrace him, yet my pride kept me back from being the loving wife God had called me to be. I allowed pride to rob me of my peace that day. *I'll* *say sorry if he says it first,* I reasoned within my mind.

Then, the Holy Spirit convicted me of this selfish mindset I had allowed myself to succumb to. He reminded me that the day I said, "I do," I was accepting the call to put my spouse's needs above my own because I no longer had only myself to think about. He reminded me of how I am now part of a covenant, one in which I am called to love my husband, even more than I love myself. Being willing to admit when you are wrong gives you the ability to place yourself in another person's shoes. When we choose to place ourselves above humility, we are robbing ourselves of so many blessings such as God-ordained relationships, inner peace, contentment, and spiritual freedom.

That night I broke down in tears. I was an imperfect woman married to an imperfect man, but God had brought us together and I was called to love him unconditionally. It is my calling as a wife to love my husband and to place the desires and necessities of my family above my own just as my husband had done for me many times before. By saying sorry that night, I granted myself inner peace.

My husband didn't have to forgive me, but he chose to. And in that, we as imperfect human beings accepted a calling way beyond ourselves, to humble ourselves and embrace our covenant just as Christ had called us to do. So today I want to encourage you to not fear using the word *sorry*. Make your wrongs right and pray that God would humble your spirit daily. We are none above humility, and we cannot walk in the godly covenant of marriage without it. I cannot stress enough how necessary of a step this is to take toward becoming a godly wife.

Daily Prayer

Heavenly Father,

I thank you for all that you are and all you are doing in my life. I recognize the calling you have placed on my life is great, and I long to bring glory and honor to your name and to abide in humility always. Help me never to become self-seeking, but keep my heart humble. Abba, show me what it means to be a woman who cloaks herself in meekness daily. Teach me how to continue walking in grace and humility.

Give me the courage to say, "I'm sorry" and to never place myself above doing so. For I recognize that the heart is deceitful, so I pray to always abide by your word and not operate on emotion. I pray that you would give me the ability to submit myself to you and to my future husband when that time comes. Cause me to become a woman who puts the needs of others before her own. Thank you, Father, for loving me, preparing me, and molding me into the future wife you have called me to be.

*In Jesus Name,
Amen*

Daily Journal

_____

_____

_____

_____

_____

_____

Scriptures to meditate on:

Matthew 5:5
Proverbs 16:19
1 Peter 3:4

Day 3: She Cherishes Wisdom

Daily Devotion

"She opens her mouth with wisdom, and the teaching of kindness is on her tongue."
Proverbs 31:26

Out of all the men and women in the Bible, God calls King Solomon the wisest man to ever live. In 2 Chronicles 1:8, God comes to Solomon in a dream and tells him to ask for whatever he wants and God would give it to him. Instead of asking or fame, love, money, or riches Solomon asked God for wisdom and a discerning heart to govern His people. How many of us could honestly admit we would do the same if we were in his shoes?

God was so pleased with Solomon's answer

that he not only made him the wisest man to ever live, but also gave him an abundance of wealth, possessions, and honor, more than any king before him! So my question to you is this; what is the main pursuit of your heart? Are you caught up in what you can gain in this life or is your mind focused on things above?

    Wisdom must become our main pursuit. Wisdom gives us the ability to know which path in life to take, and the ability to discern right from wrong. Wisdom is what will save you and keep you as you wait for your Boaz. Wisdom is what is going to keep you in a loving and faithful marriage once the wedding is all said and done. Wisdom is the most valuable tool that you can apply to every aspect of your life, and all you have to do is ask God for it. James 1:5 tells us that if we lack wisdom, we must ask God and He will gladly give it to us. Wisdom is so important to use when making decisions concerning marriage. Ask Abba's opinion in every matter and pray for discernment to know His will for your life, then trust that He will guide your every step.

    Today I want to challenge you to examine where your heart is. Place wisdom before money, fame, possessions, and followers. How can we apply wisdom to our lives? Ask yourself this; am I gentle, pure, full of peace, reasonable, full of good fruit, full of mercy, impartial, and sincere? If so, it is evident that you are applying heavenly wisdom to your life according to James 3:17. Strive to become a woman of wisdom today, because this will make such a huge difference in your heart now as a single woman falling in love with Jesus and will impact your future in more ways than you can even realize.

Daily Prayer

Heavenly Father,

I pray that you would let no corrupt talk come out of my mouth but that I would cherish wisdom and pursue peace all the days of my life. I pray that you would give me the discernment to know your will for my life and that I would use your guidance in every decision I make. I pray you would give me the wisdom to not only wait for my Boaz, but to apply it to my season of singleness, as well as when you call me to the role of a wife.

When the time comes, I will embrace my husband with kindness, humility, and peace. Help me to bring him good, not harm all the days of his life. Help us to both walk in wisdom each step of the way before and after you bring us together. I pray that you would cause my heart to be upright and without fault. Father, I long to become more gentle, pure, peaceful, reasonable, merciful, full of good fruit, impartial, and sincere. Mold me into the woman you have called me to be and show me how to apply heavenly wisdom to every aspect of my life.

In Jesus name,
Amen

Daily Journal

_____

_____

_____

_____

_____

_____

_____

_____

_____

_____

_____

Scriptures to meditate on:

Proverbs 2:6
James 3:17
Proverbs 16:16

Day 4: She Exemplifies Generosity

Daily Devotion

"She opens her hand to the poor and reaches out her hands to the needy. She is not afraid of snow for her household, for all her household are clothed in scarlet."
Proverbs 31:20-21

I once heard a startling statement from a man preaching on television many years ago. He preached a message on giving, and made a claim that if every single church member in the world gave a ten percent tithe and that it was used in accordance with Biblical standards, that there would not be one starving child in the world today. I cannot recall one other thing the preacher said, but that statement alone struck a chord in my heart.

We cannot take our materialistic possessions to the grave with us. Everything we've acquired in our lifetime is because of God, therefore it never belonged to us anyway. Still yet, it is so easy to define our worth and success by our financial status because we have been conditioned by our society to do so. Many of us attempt to store up treasures here on earth because of our underlying fear of the unforeseeable future. But the birds of the air do not fret about what they are going to eat and drink, and neither does the daughter who knows her Papa will provide all of her needs. She trusts God to keep her safe, even in her most difficult times. This type of woman, the one who places her full trust in God, is able to cheerfully extend her hand to the needy and become the heart of God to those who have been battered.

You can also apply this same concept to marriage. God is the giver of life itself, He is also the giver of marriage. In marriage, you have to become a giver. Your calling as a wife is to put your spouse's needs before your own, and the husband is called to do the same for his wife. When both partners operate in accordance with

God's lovely plan for marriage, it creates something beautiful and astounding. Whether you are already a wife or a woman who desires wifehood one day, I encourage you to pour into those whom God has placed in your path in whatever season you are enduring. Pour into your marriage, even if you don't have one yet. Today I challenge you to put your trust in God fully, even when you do not understand. Open your heart to give of your time, love, affection, and resources. Allow God to transform your mind and trust Jehovah Jireh, the God who will provide your every need.

Daily Prayer

Heavenly Father,

I thank you for all that you have graciously given to me, even though I don't deserve it. I pray you open up doors for me to give, and that I would help others who are broken and hurting in whatever way I can and with whatever resources I have. I long to take your light to a hurting world. I pray to be your hands and feet to the wounded and battered. I want to show the love of Christ to those around me in this season. Mold me into a modern-day Proverbs 31 woman.

I also pray that you would prepare me for my future husband, and that I would approach my marriage and future husband with a generous heart, giving all that I am to my future husband. I pray that you would bless our obedience to you, and that we would lack no good thing as we continue to give out of the abundance of our hearts in whatever you have called us to do. Father, prepare me to be a godly wife who exemplifies generosity and pursues you in every season of my life.

*In Jesus name,
Amen*

Daily Journal

_____

_____

Scriptures to meditate on:

2 Corinthians 9:7
Proverbs 11:25
Luke 6:38

Day 5: She Follows Peace

Daily Devotion

"A foolish son is ruin to his father, and a wife's quarreling is a continual dripping of rain."
Proverbs 19:13

William and Alisha were once madly in love before they came to a difficult place in their marriage. William came home from work exhausted from dealing with the pressure of his demanding job and Alisha spent her days wiping little noses and playing referee with her three sons, all the while taking care of the house. As stress began to increase, William and Alisha began to allow the pressures of life to manifest in their marriage in an unhealthy way.

Instead of making their home a refuge from the chaos of the world, many days their household more so resembled a boxing ring. William was overwhelmed and needed a heart to understand, and Alisha found was longing for affection and attention, which was hard to come by considering their busy schedules. Instead of confiding in God and in each other, they both succumbed to Satan's lies that what they were longing for lied outside the covenant of their marriage. The fighting continued, and the resentment they held toward each other grew more with each passing day, eventually causing their beautiful covenant to end in a way it was never meant to end.

How would things have been different if they would have made their home a place of refuge from the chaos of this world and began to pursue peace? Marriage is not always going to be a bed of roses. Marriage is a beautiful covenant designed by God, but it also takes a lot of denying yourself and loving your spouse unconditionally. Be prepared for the quarrels, because they will surely happen. Be prepared to bicker and become frustrated, because just as you are not perfect, you cannot expect perfection from your spouse. But above all, prepared to say, "I'm sorry," and to offer a hand in peace and a heart willing to understand.

You are designed to be a safe place for your spouse. You are called to hang up the boxing gloves and pursue peace. When the time comes for God to bring along His best for you, seek refuge in your spouse and in God rather than in the things of this world when life's waves crash over you. Today I challenge you to take the necessary steps needed to become a woman who pursues peace and carries it with her everywhere she goes.

Daily Prayer

Heavenly Father,

I thank you for this day you have given me. I thank you that you are preparing me to be the kind of wife that my future husband needs. I thank you for your hand on my future and I pray you make me into a woman who pursues peace daily. Let me not stray from my destiny, but cause me to become a woman who carries peace with her everywhere she goes.

Father, I pray you deal with the things inside of me that I need to overcome. Cause me to grow and mature in the areas where I fall short. I pray that I wouldn't become imprisoned to bitterness. For I know that you have called me to hang up the boxing gloves and pursue peace, so I pray that you would show me how to become more like you. I pray that I would learn to live now in peace and harmony with those you have surrounded me with so that you can begin to prepare me for a peaceful marriage. I thank you for your hand on my future husband, and I thank you for your hand on me. I pray that when you bring your best into my life, that we would both chase after you wholeheartedly. I love you, Lord. Thank you for being so good to me.

In Jesus name,
Amen

Daily Journal

Scriptures to meditate on:

Matthew 5:9
Romans 12:18

Day 6: She Has a Servant's Heart

Daily Devotion

The LORD God said, "It is not good for the man to be alone. I will make a helper suitable for him."
Genesis 2:18

There is a beautiful passage of scripture in the thirteenth chapter of John where Jesus knows the time has come for him to be crucified. In an act of love and servitude, He bent down and washed the feet of his disciples. The disciples were astonished because they didn't understand this level of servitude being displayed by their very own Master. But in John 13:14, Jesus tells them that now He has set the example so that they should go and serve others, just as their own Master had served them. No servant is above His master so just as Jesus washed their feet, we must wash the feet of others.

We live in a culture that abides by the *every man for himself* rule. We are taught to ask, "What can I get out of this?" when approaching relationships and situations. We often use this approach even with Jesus. We often ask Him, "What can you do for me?" Instead of asking *Him* what we can do for Him out of the adoration and servitude in our hearts.

I have a daughter who loves to wear my makeup and jewelry. I tell her how beautiful she is to me, but I often remind her that as beautiful as she is on the outside, she has a beautiful heart and that is the most important thing. Becoming a woman of servitude isn't always going to be pretty. The true reflection of a beautiful heart is a woman who isn't afraid to get down on her hand and knees and get work done because she has the heart of a servant. A woman of God isn't afraid to get her hands dirty, because she knows everything that she does is unto the Lord. The same concept must be applied to marriage. You must develop a servant's heart even now in your singleness for a marriage to last. God honors the heart of a servant, and a marriage thrives when both partners give 100/100 and display the same servant's heart that our Master Jesus displayed. So my question for you today is this; How can you serve those around you during your season of waiting?

Daily Prayer

Heavenly Father,

I thank you for all that you are doing in my life. Today I pray that as I walk this road you have called me to walk, that you would give me the heart of a servant. Give me a burning passion to love and serve others, to be your hands and feet in a lost and dying world. When you see fit to bless me with the man you have for me, I pray that I would also approach marriage with that same mentality, to love and serve my husband as his helpmate.

Help me to live up to the role of what it means to be a godly wife and when I fall short, I pray you give me the grace that I need to keep going. Keep me humble, Lord, as I wait upon you. I thank you that you are preparing both my future husband and myself for our destiny and that in due time, you will bring us both together to become one. I pray that we would serve you together all the days of our life.

In Jesus name,
Amen

Daily Journal

Scriptures to meditate on:

Hebrews 6:10
Psalm 2:11

Day 7: She Embodies Strength

Daily Devotion

"My flesh and my heart may fail, But God is the strength of my heart and my portion forever."
Psalm 73:26

    I wish that I could promise you happiness from this day forward, but the reality is that even if you've been blessed with an abundance of sunshine, you're still going to have a little rain. You are still going to go through seasons in your life that are heart-wrenching and are going to test your faith. Maybe you are currently enduring one of those seasons now and feel as though you don't have the strength to keep carrying on. Regardless of what you are going through today, I want you to know that God is on your side and will never leave you. The beautiful thing about womanhood is that God created us women to be the embodiment of strength. We have the capacity to bear children, so there really isn't much we can't accomplish. We are built to persevere, to fight, and to carry on even when the odds are against us.

The strength that is inside of you is God-birthed, and you were placed here for such a time as this. You are courageous like Esther, brave like Mary, and strong like Deborah. That strength is going to see you through all the days of your life. But just remember even when you think you cannot go any further, you are not walking this road alone. God is your source of strength. He is your peace and purpose.

He has such wonderful things in store for your life, including your Boaz who will come along in His perfect timing. One day you will look back and understand why you only seen one set of footprints in the sand, and you will see all the good things you have been waiting and praying for come to pass in your life because you were strong enough to wait for them. One day, you are going to look back and sing praises for what God has done in your life and what He has delivered you from. So today, I just want to tell you to hold on sweet sister, and trust the God of strength to see you through.

Daily Prayer

Heavenly Father,

I praise you because you have made me fearfully and wonderfully. I pray that when my heart grows weary, that you would lead me to the rock that is higher than I and give me the strength to cling tightly to you and trust your plan for my life. Give me the grace to hold fast to your promises for me. I pray that you would mold me into a woman who perseveres. I thank you for making me into a woman who is the embodiment of strength. For I know you have made me courageous like Esther, brave like Mary, and strong like Deborah.

I pray that when my heart and flesh fail, that you lift me up closer to you. You are my strength and my portion. I pray that you would mold me into the wife who will be strong for her husband when his heart grows weary, and I pray that he will be strong for me as well. When we both cannot go any further, give us the wisdom to trust that you will see us through. Help us both to abide in love and walk in strength daily. I thank you for giving me the strength to wait for your best for my life.

In Jesus name,
Amen

Daily Journal

_____

_____

_____

_____

_____

_____

_____

_____

_____

_____

_____

_____

_____

Scriptures to meditate on:

Isaiah 40:29-31
Philippians 4:13

Day 8: She Walks in Excellence

Daily Devotion

"An excellent wife, who can find? For her worth is far above jewels."
Proverbs 31:10

An excellent wife is the crown of her husband, but becoming one isn't accomplished overnight or with ease. Everything you do now is preparation for becoming a godly wife, and every decision you make now will impact your future. I have been married to my husband for almost seven years, and I am still in the process of becoming a godly wife and will be until the day I leave this earth.

What does it mean to be an *excellent* wife? An excellent wife is someone whose outside appearance, no matter how beautiful, cannot even begin to compete with the beauty that is inside of her. Her character speaks for itself and no one can deny that God is on her side. She loves the broken, cares for the needy, and speaks life into the lifeless. She denies her flesh daily as she picks up her cross and follows Jesus to the ends of the earth.

    She stands beside her husband through the thick and thin and encourages him in his walk with God and ministry. She is a helper, and walks in excellence every step of the way. An excellent wife brings good to her husband, her children, her neighbors, her family, her friends, and everyone she comes in contact with. She relies on God. My beautiful friend, you and I are both a wonderful work in progress that God is molding and shaping in His likeness. We must trust the Author of our hearts to make us into a Proverbs 31 woman, who is known to be excellent and praiseworthy.

    Today I want to challenge you to take hold of the fact that God takes delight in you and has created you beautifully. Recognize His hand at work in your life, and give Him praise for all that He has done. Allow Him to mold you and fill your spirit with good things. Allow Him to transform you in His likeness and prepare you to become a godly wife.

Daily Prayer

Heavenly Father,

I praise you for all that you are. You are such a good father. Today I pray that you reveal to me what it means to be an excellent wife. I pray that I display virtue and confidence in all aspects of my life and that I would walk forth into all that you have called me to do. Father, I thank you for my destiny. I thank you for my future husband's destiny. I pray that your favor over my life would flow over into my calling and future marriage.

I pray that I would have a positive impact on everyone I come in contact with, including my future husband. Help me to be his backbone and helpmate. Cause my heart to become more and more beautiful with each day. Teach me the true meaning of what beauty is in your eyes. Mold me, purify me, teach me, and shape me into the woman you have called me to be and prepare my heart for my future husband.

In Jesus name,
Amen

Daily Journal

_____

_____

_____

_____

_____

_____

_____

Scriptures to meditate on:

Titus 2:7
2 Corinthians 8:7
2 Peter 1:3-4

Day 9: She is Virtuous

Daily Devotion

"The heart of her husband trusts in her, and he will have no lack of gain. She does him good and not evil All the days of her life."
Proverbs 31:11-12

As intimate beings, we desire friendship. We want someone we can depend on and trust with even our deepest secrets. Before I married my sweetheart, I was convinced that I had what it took to be the wife he needed. I was so confident in myself, but then there came days where depression and anxiety flooded my heart, and it felt like everything that could go wrong in my life, went wrong. I felt unstable, shaken to my core, and fell short time and time again of what it meant to be a *trustworthy* wife. I had come to a point in my life where if I had just one anxiety attack that day, I considered it a good day.

The doctors diagnosed me with PTSD and postpartum anxiety after developing severe preeclampsia and bringing my little girl into the world nine weeks too early. During this time in my life I became angry at myself and everyone around me, and I pushed away the ones I loved most because of the gut-wrenching pain I was experiencing. Instead of allowing my pain to define me any longer, I began to cling that much tighter to God and to my husband. By allowing God to take my pain and give it purpose, I displayed virtue in the midst of my grieving.

A wise woman once told me, "Tiffany, just know that the hard times will come. When they do, remember that your husband is on the same team as you so you *must* fight alongside each other, not *with* each other." I held onto that piece of wisdom so that I can now pass it onto you; when the hard times come, be a wife in whom your husband can trust and marry the man who will do the same for you.

Don't allow the enemy to use those times to plant seeds of disunity or confusion. Instead, cling to one another and to Jesus. Pain is no respecter of persons and can bring out the worst in people, but when you place your trust in Jesus, He will enable you to be the woman and future wife that you need to be. Cling to God's love for you and He will show you how to become a woman of virtue.

Daily Prayer

Heavenly Father,

I thank you for all that you are doing in my life as you prepare me for wifehood and my calling. I strive to be a cornerstone for my future husband. Make me into a wife that my future husband can place his full trust in no matter what may come in this life. Cause me to be a blessing to the man I marry so that I can bring him good, not harm, all the days of his life. I pray that he would find in me exactly what he needs.

Embed in me a trustworthy spirit. Help me to display virtue in both the good and bad times. Fashion me into a woman who is a blessing to everyone she comes in contact with. I pray to be a friend in whom others can confide to everyone you have placed in my path from this moment on. Help me to hold true to all that you have called me to be and to cling tightly to you in every season of my life.

In Jesus name,
Amen

Daily Journal

_____

_____

_____

_____

_____

_____

Scriptures to meditate on:

1 John 2:5-6
Luke 16:10

Day 10: She Models Grace

Daily Devotion

"A gracious woman attains honor, but ruthless men gain only wealth."
Proverbs 11:16

Grace is one of the simplest concepts, yet our human nature cannot fathom its simplicity so we tend to overcomplicate it. The beautiful thing about grace is that we can never escape its reach. Given that small, simple truth, just as God has been gracious to us, we must extend grace to others in the same manner. Every single day, you will come in contact with grace whether you are extending or receiving it.

In my marriage, I cannot begin to count how many times I've needed grace from my husband,

and how many times he has needed it from me. If grace doesn't become a part of your daily routine in a marriage, it will not make it. Grace has to become deeply embedded in the roots of a marriage for it to last. But grace cannot only be a part of your marriage, it must become a part of your daily walk in Christ. Just as you were forgiven, you must forgive others. Matthew 8:21-22 tells us this, "Then Peter came to Jesus and asked, "Lord, how many times shall I forgive my brother who sins against me? Up to seven times?" Jesus answered, "I tell you, not just seven times, but seventy-seven times!"

Grace must become a part of us. We must examine our hearts daily and rid ourselves of any bitterness or ill intention. Ask the Lord to test and try your heart, and to help you to demonstrate grace in your future marriage and your walk with Him. When you take hold of grace and begin to operate in it daily, you are setting yourself free and preparing your heart for the beautiful future God has in store for you. Grace will impact your life and everyone around you, so my challenge to you today is this; become a woman who models grace and you will begin to watch chains fall off of you.

Daily Prayer

Heavenly Father,

I pray that you reveal to me what it means to be a woman who walks in the unmerited favor of God. I pray your favor and grace over my future husband's life and my life. Help me to demonstrate grace daily in every aspect of my life. Teach me to extend grace to others and to myself, because I know that you have called me to embrace forgiveness just as you have forgiven me.

I pray that you mold and shape me into a gracious woman. Make me into a woman who holds her head high despite what life throws her way. Give me strength to face each day with the grace you have given me. Thank you for loving me, molding me, and showing me grace that I cannot earn and don't deserve. I pray that the grace you have poured into my life will flow through me into the lives of everyone around me. I pray that when you bring along your best for me, that I will extend grace daily to my future husband and love him unconditionally.

In Jesus name,
Amen

Daily Journal

_____

_____

_____

_____

_____

_____

_____

Scriptures to meditate on:

Colossians 4:6
Psalm 101:2

Day 11: She is a Helpmate

Daily Devotion

"Wives, be subject to your husbands, as is fitting in the Lord."
Colossians 3:18

Biblical submission is one of the most controversial topics in the entire Bible. Our world has so badly warped our perception on what biblical submission in marriage actually means. biblical submission is not a dictatorship, and it is never an excuse to control your partner. Biblical submission, I believe, is a mutual love and respect for each other. Ephesians 5:21 even tells us to submit to one another out of reverence for Christ.

    A godly man will nurture you, love you, and give you the confidence to trust in him as the head of the family. It is important to understand that submission can only be accomplished when the husband is like Christ and loves His wife in such a way that he would die daily for her. When a wife is loved and cared for in such a way, she will have no problem with submission. How can I be my husband's helpmate? I love him, support him, and pray for him. Being a helpmate means fulfilling your spouse's physical, spiritual, emotional, mental, and sexual needs.

A loving, sensitive husband will not force his wife to do anything against God's will, and he will not push her into anything distasteful or harmful to her. Submission never means being a doormat, and a godly husband will not degrade his wife, but rather, he will treat her like his queen. The husband does not make decisions that contradict the needs of his family and will never assert authority to get his own way. He lives in such a way that he dies to self and lays down his life for his family daily. When both individuals operate in their calling the way they were meant too, both partners will be fulfilled and bring glory to God.

So today my beautiful sister, I encourage you to use discernment in praying for and choosing a partner. Wait for the man who will love you just as Christ loves His bride. Ask God to show you what it means to be a helpmate and to prepare you to become the wife your future husband needs.

Daily Prayer

Heavenly Father,

In a world that often tends to stray away from your ideas on marriage and love, I pray that you would cause me to be a wife who is a helpmate to her future husband. I pray that you would mold me into a wife who loves, honors, and respects her husband. Help me to encourage him in every way that I can and give him unconditional love when you bring us together.

Rid me of my pride and selfishness. Keep me on the path you have called me to travel. I want to be a woman and wife after your own heart who blesses everyone she comes in contact with. Give me discernment in praying for and choosing a partner. Save my heart only for the man you have for me, who will love me deeply and is a reflection of you. Teach me what biblical submission means as I walk this journey with you. Thank you for all that you are doing in my future husband's life and in mine. Thank you for your amazing love.

In Jesus name,
Amen

Daily Journal

_____

_____

_____

_____

_____

_____

Scriptures to meditate on:

Genesis 2:18
Ephesians 5:25
1 Corinthians 11:3

Day 12: She Embraces Intimacy

Daily Devotion

"For this reason a man shall leave his father and his mother, and be joined to his wife; and they shall become one flesh."
Genesis 2:24

For better or for worse, for richer or for poorer, in sickness and in health, to love and to cherish, till death do us part. We proudly exclaim these vows with good intentions on our wedding day, but do we really grasp onto their meaning? God did not intend for our mindset approaching marriage to be *if it doesn't work out I can always just get a divorce.* Marriage is a higher calling way beyond ourselves and bids us to abolish all selfishness. The person God has for us isn't placed in your life simply to make you happy. Your spouse is your battle partner, someone who will challenge you spiritually and help you to grow in your walk with God and ministry. Your spouse is your God-ordained partner to grow, build, and learn with. Marriage is not for the self-serving. In marriage you will face hardships, but the more you embrace intimacy with your spouse and cling tightly to him, the more you will become in tune with one another and with God's will for your life.

    You can embrace intimacy with your future spouse even now in your season of singleness by praying and waiting. When God brings along His best for you, don't allow anything or anyone in this world to sow discord in your marriage or mind. Keep God first, and your spouse second. Today I want to encourage you to allow God to transform your ideology on what intimacy is. I pray the Holy Spirit would reveal His love and heart for intimacy in marriage to you. Don't give the enemy any foothold in your life or future marriage and keep your mind pure. Remember that a cord of three strands is not so easily broken. Tie yourself to God, then tie yourself to your husband. Don't let anything unravel you from God or your spouse. Stay consistent in prayer, grace, love, and the word of God as you prepare and wait.

Daily Prayer

Heavenly Father,

I thank you for the work you are doing in my life. I pray that when the time is right, you help both my husband and I to cleave to one another and to embrace intimacy in our marriage and walk with you. Help me to prepare now for marriage by praying for my future husband and becoming the kind of wife he needs. I pray that we would always keep you at the center of our marriage and truly grasp the meaning of the vows we recite on our wedding day.

Let us place the needs of each other above our own. Help us to walk closely to one another and to you. I thank you that you are preparing both of our hearts to come together in due time. I thank you for loving and cherishing me. Above all, Lord, I want to embrace intimacy with you and draw closer to you.

In Jesus name,
Amen

Daily Journal

_____

_____

_____

_____

_____

_____

_____

_____

_____

_____

_____

_____

_____

_____

_____

Scriptures to meditate on:

Ephesians 5:33
Hebrews 13:4
Genesis 2:24

Day 13: She Exemplifies Inner Beauty

Daily Devotion

"Your beauty should not come from outward adornment, such as elaborate hairstyles and the wearing of gold jewelry or fine clothes. Rather, it should be that of your inner self, the unfading beauty of a gentle and quiet spirit, which is of great worth in God's sight."
1 Peter 3:3-4

Just as the Apostle Paul said, the woman whose heart radiates from the inside out captures the heart of the King. You are a daughter of the Most High, and He looks on you with amazement and adoration because He created you so beautifully. A woman of God embraces modesty both externally and internally because she has found her worth and identity in Christ. She knows who she is and knows that she is *enough* just the way God created her. She knows she doesn't have to bear all for attention because she isn't trying to attract the wrong man, she's looking to attract her Boaz.

I want you to take notice of the fact that when Paul is *not* saying we as women should not fix up or make an effort to look beautiful if that is what we desire. But what he *is* saying is that as a woman of God, your looks and outward appearance should not even begin to touch the surface in comparison with what is in your heart. Let your heart be the most beautiful thing about you. Embrace gentleness and kindness, for that is far more beautiful than any piece of clothing or makeup you will ever find.

The man God has for you will be captivated by your inner beauty. While he will appreciate your outward beauty, what will truly capture his heart is your beautiful spirit. If a man only sees you for what you look like on the outside, he is not the man God has for you. You will not find a godly man chasing after a woman who is in search of attention. He is looking to see God in her, not at her physical form. Real attracts real, so rest in the fact knowing that God is preparing both you and your future husband and in His perfect timing, He will bring you both together. So today, my beautiful sister, embrace the stunning treasure that you are and allow God to reveal your incredible worth to you.

Daily Prayer

Heavenly Father,

In a culture that convinces me that I must reveal all to get a man, I pray you help me to rise above and be the woman you have called me to be. I pray that you would give me the ability to save my pearls, that I wouldn't cast them before swine. Help me to save my heart, body, and mind for my future husband, and I pray that you save him for me as well.

Father help me to embrace the fact that you love me and call me your treasure. I pray to always pursue your beauty in everything that I do.

In a superficial world, I pray that you shift my focus toward pursuing inner beauty, which is of great worth in your sight. Give me a gentle spirit, and show me the meaning of true beauty in your eyes. I thank you for your beauty, grace, and unconditional love for me.

In Jesus name,
Amen

Daily Journal

_____

_____

_____

_____

_____

_____

Scriptures to meditate on:

Ephesians 2:10
Romans 12:2
1 Peter 5:5

Day 14: She Abides in Gratitude

Daily Devotion

"And whatever you do, in word or deed, do everything in the name of the Lord Jesus, giving thanks to God the Father through him."
Colossians 3:17

If we are not careful, we will spend an entire lifetime wishing for the things we do not yet have. So often I myself am guilty of this, so today I want to encourage you not to wish one more minute of your precious life away. We must carry hope with us. In fact, Proverbs 13:12 tells us, "hope deferred makes the heart sick." We must hope and pray for the good things God has in store for our lives, but we must also embrace right where we are because today is a day you will never get back. If we do not guard our hearts diligently, discontentment will sneak in and rob us of today's joy. Discontentment will rob you of everything good in your life if you allow it too. But we can fight discontentment by digging up the things in our heart that shouldn't be there and replacing them with good things.

There are many roots of discontentment, so today I want to challenge you to find the cause of those roots, dig them up, and plant seeds of thankfulness and gratitude. You don't have to worry about your future because God already has it written in the palm of his hand. And if God is already there, you can bet it's going to be something wonderful. Bitterness, envy, and anxiety breed discontentment, but thankfulness breeds contentment. Gratitude will overflow into every area of your life including your future marriage.

Practice thankfulness in this moment, no matter what your situation may be. Just as the apostle Paul spoke about in Philippians 4:8, set your minds on whatever is true, noble, right, pure lovely, honorable, admirable, excellent, and praiseworthy.

Don't allow discontentment to rob you of

today's blessings. If you are discontent now in your singleness, you will be discontent when you are married. There needs to be a heart change that takes place for you to embrace the life and marriage God has called you too. And trust me when I say this; you don't want to allow anything to rob you of the incredible future God has in store for you.

Daily Prayer

Heavenly Father,

Today I pray that you would cause my heart to overflow with gratitude for all that you have given me. Thankfulness breeds contentment, and I pray that an abundance of thankfulness would dwell in my heart. I thank you Abba for all that you are doing in my life and all you have done for me.

Fashion me into a woman who abides in gratitude all the days of her life. Help me to combat the lies of the enemy with prayer and thankfulness. I thank you for what you are doing in my life and in my future husband's life. I know that in due time you will bring both of our hearts together to love and serve you. I pray that my heart would remain full of love and contentment right now during my singleness as well as in marriage. Thank you for the peace that only you can give and for your overwhelming love for me.

In Jesus name,
Amen

Daily Journal

_____

_____

_____

_____

Scriptures to meditate on:

1 Thessalonians 5:18
Colossians 3:15
Philippians 4:6

Day 15: She Cherishes Joy

Daily Devotion

"This day is holy to our Lord. Do not grieve, for the joy of the LORD is your strength."
Nehemiah 8:10

Today you can make the decision to allow the hurt and pain that you've been through to engulf your heart or you can get up, dust yourself off, and walk forward boldly into your destiny. The promise God gives us in Nehemiah 8:10 is a promise that you can carry with you all the days of your life, that the joy of the Lord is your strength. Today you can choose the joy of the Lord over your current circumstance. We all have times when life just gets to even the best of us. It's okay to mourn and grieve, in fact it is necessary, but we must come to the place where we must allow Abba to transform our mind in His likeness, so that we may walk daily in love, peace, joy, and strength. The enemy loves to remind us of who we used to be. But you can combat his tactics by praising God for where He has brought you from.

Sometimes, even in prayer, I will be reminded of an incident from the past that hurt me. But instead of dwelling in the pain of yesterday, God has taught me to shift my focus to where He has brought me and where He is taking me. We have to come through trials in our life to produce perseverance, character, and hope. But we don't have to live in past hurts and allow the enemy to rob us of today's joy. You are a new creature in Christ and your peace is an important component for where God is taking you.

Don't let hurtful memories plant a seed of bitterness in your heart. Hold onto your peace and be thankful you're not where you used to be. So today I challenge you, allow God to take that hurt and pain that has been causing your spirit to feel unsettled and replace it with the joy and strength that only He can give. You are going to make it through sweet sister. Always remember who the source of your strength is.

Daily Prayer

Heavenly Father,

I thank you Lord for the unspeakable joy and peace that only you can give. Protect my heart from discouragement, and use me to encourage others to walk in joy and peace. Heal my heart of past hurts and rejections. Show me the love you have for me and that you have a beautiful future in store for me. Help me to give my pain to you so that you can bring beauty from my ashes.

I pray to bring joy to my future husband when you see fit to bring us together. I pray that we would both abide in joy and encourage one another. Father I thank you that my cup overflows and that you are my strength. Strengthen my spirit, and protect my heart, Lord. Your joy is our strength and I love you endlessly.

In Jesus name,
Amen

Daily Journal

_____

_____

_____

_____

_____

Scriptures to meditate on:

James 1:2
Romans 15:13
Romans 14:17

Day 16: She Walks in Love

Daily Devotion

"Love is patient and kind; love does not envy or boast; it is not arrogant or rude. It does not insist on its own way; it is not irritable or resentful; it does not rejoice at wrongdoing, but rejoices with the truth."
1 Corinthians 13:4-6

In 1 Corinthians 13:13, Paul makes a rather bold statement by saying that love is the greatest quality one can possess, even more so than hope or faith. But why is love the greatest? Just as faith without works is dead, so is our walk without love. The true mark of a believer is someone who has been completely changed by the One who is love, so the fruit they bear all stems from love. The woman who has fallen head over heels in love with God has discovered the truest love there is. Because she has experienced the reckless love of Jesus, she is able to love others genuinely. This kind of love pours over into every relationship in her life. Everywhere she goes she proves to be a blessing, not a curse. She is an encourager who walks in blessings. She can love others sufficiently because she knows that she is loved perfectly by her Father.

    We must learn to fall in love with God and be a reflection of His love to others. His love beckons us to look past the exterior and into the heart. Divine love will enable you to see the diamond in the rough and the treasure behind the dust. In order to fully love your future husband the way you were designed to, you must first come to know and experience the indescribable love of God. So today, I want to challenge you to fall in love with God and allow His love to cleanse, heal, and renew you. Walk in love. Today, go forth and be the love of Jesus to someone who needs Him.

Daily Prayer

Heavenly Father,

I thank you for your wondrous love for me. I want to fall more in love with you, Jesus. Fashion me into a woman is an example of your love to others. I want to take the light of your love into a lost and dying world. Let them see you in me. Help me to follow the example you have given me in 1 Corinthians 13 of what love is. Help me to become more patient and kind. Help me to become less envious, boastful, proud, and self-seeking.

I pray that when I feel overwhelmed by the pressures of this world, that I would be reminded of the love you have for me. I want to be a woman and wife who carries love with her everywhere she goes. I pray that my love for you would pour over into all of my relationships. I love you so much Abba.

In Jesus name,
Amen

Daily Journal

_____

_____

_____

_____

Scriptures to meditate on:

Hebrews 13:1
James 3:17
1 John 5:2

Day 17: She Follows Mercy

Daily Devotion

"You have heard that it was said, 'You shall love your neighbor and hate your enemy.' But I say to you, love your enemies and pray for those who persecute you, so that you may be sons of your Father who is in heaven.
Matthew 5:43-45

When we are hurt, it can be so easy to focus on our pain and forget the times in our own life that we desperately needed mercy. When your heart is ruled by bitterness, becoming a woman of mercy can be a daunting task. If you are anything like me, you may struggle with wanting to hold onto the past. The beautiful thing about Jesus is that he casts our sins as far as the east is from the west. His love enables us to forgive. He gives mercy to the merciless and forgives us daily, even though we don't deserve it.

How would our lives be changed if we began to reflect our beautiful Jesus and embrace mercy? Jesus calls us to rid ourselves of all bitterness, envy, hatred, and selfishness. He is calling us to die to self and begin to love how he loves. He has set the ultimate example for us. Matthew 6:15 tells us if we do not forgive men of their trespasses against us, our Heavenly Father will not forgive us. Therefore, it is evident that God calls us to be forgivers and to literally dismiss any offense that may come our way.

Forgiveness isn't for the other person, forgiveness is for you. Forgiveness is the key that will set you free. Today, I challenge you to ask Abba to test your heart and bring to the light any offensive way that is in you. For where you are going you can't pack any excess baggage, so let go of the bitterness and pain today and follow mercy into your destiny.

Daily Prayer

Heavenly Father,

Have mercy on me because I am a sinner in need of grace. I pray that you would help me to become a forgiver who embraces mercy, whether I am extending or receiving it. Rid my heart of all bitterness and hurt so that I can be free to follow you wherever you may lead.
Help me to show mercy, just as it has been shown to me. I desire to be a walking, talking example of Christ. Fashion me into a woman who loves others the way you love them. I pray that I would not only become a woman established in grace and mercy, but that I would also be a merciful wife when you bring along your best for me. I thank you for your love and grace Papa.

In Jesus name,
Amen

Prayer Journal

_____

_____

_____

_____

_____

Scriptures to meditate on:

Luke 6:36
Psalm 23:6

Day 18: She Embraces Compassion

Daily Devotion

"Religion that is pure and undefiled before God, the Father, is this: to visit orphans and widows in their affliction, and to keep oneself unstained from the world."
James 1:27

Our society has taught us to abide by two rules in order to be successful. The first rule is to fend for ourselves and the second is to look out for number one, both of which go against God's command to love our neighbor as ourselves. As women of God, we must set ourselves apart from the ways of this world. The woman who embraces compassion chooses not to conform to the patterns of this world but allows God to renew and transform her mind. As women who love Jesus, we must show compassion and mercy in the face of injustice. We mustn't fear what the future holds, because we trust that God will always provide our every need. Due to this favor we've received from God, we are able to go into the world and make a difference. We are able to embrace those around us and show them the love of God. A compassionate woman is a beautiful phenomenon.

    We must pray that God would test our hearts and show any offensive way in us. Ask God to give you eyes to see the things He sees, and a heart to love people the way He loves them. Compassion goes a long way. One spark of compassion in a person's life has the capability to start a forest fire that could change the entire world. Compassion is also a necessary component in marriage. In order for a marriage to last, you have to become a forgiver. You have to embrace selflessness and show mercy daily, and the only way to do that is to rely fully on God every step of the way. A woman who embraces compassion has learned to put herself in another person's shoes and to not always assume the worst. She sympathizes with others. She is able to show compassion because she has been through places in her life where she has needed mercy. So today I challenge you, woman of God, to embrace compassion with everything in you. Let it flow from your heart into every relationship of your life, including your future marriage.

Daily Prayer

Heavenly Father,

I thank you for the calling you have placed on my life. I pray that you would mold me into a woman who looks after the needs of others and places them above her own. I pray that you would abolish all selfishness in my heart, because I know that selflessness is important for a marriage to last.

I want to love others the way you love them, Abba. Cause compassion to blossom abundantly in my heart. Give me eyes to see what you see, and a heart to love people the way you love them. Give me eager hands and swift feet to reach the lost. Root and establish me in love, so that I may reach others and carry that selflessness in contact with everyone I meet, including my future husband when you see fit.

*In Jesus name,
Amen*

Daily Journal

_____

_____

_____

_____

_____

_____

_____

_____

_____

_____

_____

_____

_____

Scriptures to meditate on:

Philippians 2:1-3
Psalm 119:156
Psalm 145:9

Day 19: She is Faithful

Daily Devotion

"He who is faithful in what is least is faithful also in much; and he who is unjust in what is least is unjust also in much."
Luke 16:10

Being faithful in marriage means sticking it out even when you are hurt, angry, and long to be ruled by your emotions. The heart can be a precarious thing. Jeremiah 17:9 even tells us, "the heart is deceitful above all things without a cure. Who can understand it?"

Surely Jeremiah had at least once in his life been ruled by his heart only to find himself utterly deceived, because he felt it necessary to warn us. It's easy to make rash decisions and say things we don't particularly mean when we are ruled by our feelings, but God is calling us to mature and grow emotionally and spiritually, and allow our hearts to be dictated solely by the word of God.

    After I had my daughter, I'm pretty sure I made the list for top 10 most emotional women on this planet. For months I was not myself, and found it hard to rationalize how I felt due to the postpartum anxiety and depression that was clouding my heart and mind. I wanted to push my husband away. I wanted to push *everyone* away. Anything, no matter how small or insignificant in the grand scheme of things, sent me over the edge in a frenzy. During that time in my life I found it hard to connect with God and my husband. There were times I wanted to throw in the towel on both my relationship with my husband and even with God out of anger and hurt, but today I am glad that God revealed to me how I was allowing my heart to be ruled by my circumstance and emotions.

    I began to come back to the word of God, and He began to mature my heart spiritually and emotionally all the while revealing His love for me once again. I chose cling tighter to God and my husband as He did His work in my heart, so that I could love my husband and Him more fiercely and faithfully. A woman of God chooses to be ruled by the word of God and the covenant she has made between God and her husband rather than by her emotions. My hope is that you will take away this today; the heart can be deceitful, so grow in the word of God and rely on Him fully because that is what is going to bring the growth and maturity you need. In doing this, you are setting yourself up for a future filled with blessings because you chose to remain faithful.

Daily Prayer

Heavenly Father,

I thank you for all that you are and all that you are doing in my life. Today I pray that you would work on me, and correct any commitment issues that may lie within me. Help me to become faithful in the small things so that I can soon be faithful in more substantial things. I pray that every seed I have sowed in faithfulness will reap an abundant harvest.

Dig up everything that is unpleasant in your sight, Lord. Test and try my heart that I would prove faithful to you above all others. Cause my heart to mature emotionally and spiritually. Help me to become a better woman with each passing day. I pray that you would establish me in faithfulness now in this season of waiting for my future husband and when the time comes for me to marry the man you have for me. I love you Father.

In Jesus name,
Amen

Daily Journal

_____

_____

_____

_____

_____

_____

_____

_____

_____

_____

_____

Scriptures to meditate on:

Deuteronomy 29:9
Hosea 2:20
Isaiah 54:5

Day 20: She Walks in Forgiveness

Daily Devotion

"And when you stand praying, if you hold anything against anyone, forgive them, so that your Father in heaven may forgive you your sins."
Mark 11:25

Forgiveness has always been and still is one of the great obstacles that I face in my walk with God. Forgiveness forces us to look into the deepest parts of a person and see them with spiritual eyes rather than through worldly eyes. Forgiveness forces us to reflect on the times we didn't deserve grace, yet God freely granted it to us. Forgiveness boldly exclaims, "Father, forgive them! For they know not what they do," whereas bitterness tempts us to focus only our ourselves and the pain they afflicted.

It is hard to let go of an offense. It is even harder to forgive when your heart is broken into pieces. But forgiveness is essential to your growth. You cannot hold onto bitterness and expect God to bring you into your destiny. You have to keep moving forward. You have to let go for the sake of your soul. You have a purpose and so many good things in store for you, so don't let it be bitterness that holds you captive. You are not a prisoner, you have been set free and now heir with Christ Jesus.

Overcome bitterness and pain now, so that it won't negatively affect the marriage God has for you. There is going to come a time you are going to need to forgive your spouse. Likewise, there will be times when you will be the one in need of forgiveness because we have all sinned and fell short of the glory of God. We must forgive others just as we have been forgiven. When you learn to forgive, you really grasp onto the revelation that forgiveness isn't really for the other person, forgiveness is for you.

Daily Prayer

Heavenly Father,

I thank you for the grace you give me daily even though I don't deserve it. I pray that you would mature my heart so that when an offense is made against me, that I would respond with love and grace. Remove all bitterness, envy, and strife from my heart. Fashion me into an example of your love everywhere I go. Cause my heart to be set on fire for you. You have forgiven me, so I know that I must extend grace to others.

Forgiveness can sometimes be such a daunting task for me, but I know that it plays an essential role in shaping me into the woman and wife that you desire for me to be. Help me to pursue holiness each day and to walk in your ways. Help me to embrace love, grace, mercy, and peace all the days of my life. Thank you for loving and cherishing me. Thank you for preparing me to be the wife my future husband needs.

In Jesus name,

Amen

Daily Journal

_____

_____

_____

_____

_____

_____

_____

_____

_____

_____

_____

_____

_____

_____

Scriptures to meditate on:

Colossians 3:13
Luke 17:3-4
Ephesians 4:31-32

Day 21: She Dwells in Integrity

Daily Devotion

"He who walks with integrity walks securely, but he who perverts his ways will become known."
Proverbs 10:9

Integrity means to hold fast to strong moral principles. Woman of the word look, act, and speak different from women of the world. The key to dwelling in integrity is to pray before taking any step in your life. Prayer is the key to a Christian's walk with God, and it is especially important to use when making decisions. When you abide in prayer and discernment, God will keep your foot from slipping as you follow His lead.

The harsh reality is that the enemy is still at

work in people's lives. With that being said, people may still lie on you, try to manipulate you, and try to ruin your reputation. They did it to Jesus, and we are certainly not above Him. But when you are a woman who dwells in integrity, who you are will shine through and God will shed light on the darkness.

In the end, all of the weapons and tactics the enemy used against you will shatter and be exposed. Practice integrity, beautiful woman of God, now in your season of waiting and when God brings you into the holy covenant of marriage. Integrity will attract God's best for you. The man that God has set aside for you isn't looking for a woman of the world.

A true Boaz looks for a woman of the word, a woman who walks in integrity daily. He will see you as the treasure that you are and embrace your worth. So don't waste your time on boys. Wait for the *man* God has promised you and dwell in integrity in your current season and the seasons to come.

Daily Prayer

Heavenly Father,

I thank you for what you are doing in my life. Prepare me to be the kind of woman who asks your opinion before taking a step. I pray that I would become a godly example to other women around me, and that I would walk in integrity daily. I want to follow your lead, Lord. Give me the courage to maintain integrity in all of my relationships and walk with you. Prepare and mold my heart as I walk this narrow road.

Papa, I thank you for your love. I thank you for showing me that I am your treasure and that you take great delight in me. Mold me into a woman of the word. Keep me steadfast as I wait on the man you have called me to marry. Help us to both maintain integrity together as a couple when you see fit to bring us together.

In Jesus name,
Amen

Daily Journal

_____

_____

_____

_____

_____

Scriptures to meditate on:

Proverbs 11:3
Proverbs 21:3
Hebrews 13:18

Day 22: She Has Unshakable Faith

Daily Devotion

"Therefore know that the Lord your God, He is God, the faithful God who keeps covenant and mercy for a thousand generations with those who love Him and keep His commandments;"
Deuteronomy 7:9

What is holding you back from receiving all that God has in store for you? What promises have you been struggling to hold onto? Matthew 17:20 tells us that if we even had faith the size of a mustard seed, we can tell any mountain to move and it will move. But often times our inability to see the world around us with spiritual eyes cause us to have doubt in our hearts.

If you struggle with faith, take heart. It doesn't mean God is mad at you, it means you are a human in need of grace, the exact reason Christ died on the cross for our sins.

Many things may hinder us from remaining steadfast in our faith. But what we can do is ask God to uncover our spiritual eyes and deepen our faith in Him, then trust that He will. Faith teaches us to grasp onto the spiritual even while residing in our earthly flesh. God not only loves us divinely, but he longs to bless us and sometimes it's just a matter of simply asking Papa God to align your heart with His and to bless you with the desires of your heart.

Pray God's will over your life then have faith that He will do what He said He will do. Faith does not operate on your timetable, but rather on God's. So today, whether you are praying for your future husband or just long to deepen your walk with Christ, I encourage you to put your trust fully in Christ, and ask Him to reveal whatever may be holding you back from growing in your faith. Just remember, if you have faith even the size of a mustard seed, you have the ability to move any mountain in your life.

Daily Prayer

Heavenly Father,

Daily my faith is tested. I pray that you would raise up a standard against the enemy and let faith arise in my heart, Lord. Help me to walk in faith and to rely fully on you, even when I can't see the road that is before me. I know that you are a good father and I will trust you, no matter what lies ahead of me.

Strengthen my faith. Help me to hold fast to my faith in you as I walk into the purpose and destiny you have called me to. I long to receive every good thing you have in store for me so if my faith must be tested, I will fight the good fight in order to see a brighter tomorrow. Help me to hold onto the promises you have made for me and to trust in you every step of the way. Thank you for your beautiful love for me.

In Jesus name,
Amen

Daily Journal

_____

_____

_____

_____

_____

_____

Scriptures to meditate on:

1 John 5:5
Galatians 2:20
John 6:35

Day 23: She Encourages

Daily Devotion

"Therefore comfort each other and edify one another, just as you also are doing."
1 Thessalonians 5:11

I am an encourager, you can ask my husband. I feel as though my calling in life is to encourage and speak into the lives of those around me, but one of the most difficult tasks I have found is that when you are discouraged, it becomes very difficult to operate as an *encourager.*

Over the last couple of months my husband and I have been on a fitness journey. Recently I hit a plateau where my weight would not budge, all the while my husband would move from one side of the house to the other and lose about five pounds. About two months ago I stepped on the scale only to discover I weighed exactly the same as I did one month ago. I become so frustrated and felt like my efforts were in vain. I huffed and puffed all the way to my closet to throw on my fat pants and go buy myself some chocolate.

It took me an entire week to get back on track, and I'm lucky it only took that long. Likewise, if you allow discouragement into your heart, it can actually cause you to go backward instead of forward. Slow progress is still progress, whether it has to do with your health, career, or family.

Something that is amazing about God is he knows exactly what we need and when we need it. He places people and things in our life to encourage and keep us going. But it is also our job to keep ourselves encouraged in the Lord. When you get married, there will be times you will need encouragement from your husband. Then, there will be times your husband will desperately need you to encourage him. Ecclesiastes 4:10 tells us this; "Two are better than one because they have a good return for their labor. For if either of them falls, the one will lift up his companion."

So today I want to encourage you to not give up. God has a plan for your life that outweighs whatever you may be facing today. You have many new mornings ahead. You have a good purpose and a great future. You are going to be a wonderful, godly wife to a loving, godly man one day if you wait. Keep yourself encouraged and stay in the word of God.

Daily Prayer

Heavenly Father,

I thank you in advance for what you are doing in my life and the life of my future husband. I pray that you mold me into a powerful, praying wife who encourages her husband daily. I pray that you give me the strength to stand beside him and be a shoulder to lean on during hard times.
Bring us together in your perfect timing, and help us to love one another just as you have loved us. Help us to continue on the path of love before and after you bring us both together. Help me to

stay encouraged, and let me be a blessing to the man I marry. I pray that we would both lift one another up to you when you see fit to bring us together.

In Jesus name,
Amen

Daily Journal

_____

_____

_____

_____

_____

_____

Scriptures to meditate on:

Hebrews 10:24-25
1 Peter 4:8-10
1 Thessalonians 5:14

Day 24: She Clearly Communicates

Daily Devotion

"Let no corrupt word proceed out of your mouth, but what is good for necessary edification, that it may impart grace to the hearers."
Ephesians 4:29

You may have heard it said that communication is key in any relationship. There's no surprise that without communication any relationship, no matter how wonderful, can crumble to the ground. Without communication your relationship cannot stand, so today I want to challenge you with this question; when you find yourself upset or in need of something, how do you communicate your needs in order to find a logical solution? Are your efforts in doing so successful?

Many wives, and husbands too, are guilty of giving the infamous silent treatment which can be detrimental to a marriage. There are also men and women who will bottle up all of their feelings and never get to the source of the problem because they left communication out of the equation. This can cause feelings of hurt, anger, and resentment, all of which could have been avoided by just communicating in the first place. I want to encourage you today, as you go about your business, to take note of how you communicate with others and express your feelings. Ask God to reveal how you can grow in this area and how to clearly get across your wants and needs. Work on your communication skills now so that in the future you will be able to properly communicate with your spouse. A successful relationship requires two people who simply strive to be honest and open with each other about how they feel. When you love someone, you never want to leave them in the dark, and you definitely don't want to hold any part of yourself back from them and cause harm to your relationship. Communication must become a vital aspect of your life.

Daily Prayer

Heavenly Father,

I thank you for all that you are and what you are doing in my life. I thank you that one day when the time is right, you will bring along my Boaz. I pray that when that time comes, that I would be a wife who builds up my husband in love. I pray that nothing corrupt would come from my mouth, but that everything I say and do would be in love.

Help me to become a better communicator so that I can be a blessing to the man I marry. Help me to better communicate with everyone in my life. I long to clearly communicate with my future husband so that silence and miscommunicated feelings have no part in our marriage. Fashion me into a wife who builds up her husband, rather than tears him down. I pray that the words that come from my mouth would impart grace, mercy, and love always. I thank you for your hand on my life and your love for me.

In Jesus name,
Amen

Daily Journal

_____

_____

_____

_____

_____

_____

_____

_____

Scriptures to meditate on:

Ephesians 4:29
Psalm 19:14
Proverbs 12:25

Day 25: She Walks in Purity

Daily Devotion

"Do not rebuke an older man, but exhort him as a father, younger men as brothers, older women as mothers, younger women as sisters, with all purity."
Timothy 5:1-2

Did you know that what you do right now can have an impact on the rest of your life? As a single woman, I want to encourage you to seek out purity with all of your heart not only physically, but mentally as well. You can be pure physically yet filthy mentally. What do you dwell on? Where does your mind wander? Do you think about whatever is true, good, worthy, and pure? Begin this day training your mind to dwell on things above. Purity is underrated in today's world. I want to encourage you to not look at every available man in your life as a potential *Boaz*, but rather, view them as a brother in the Lord. Allow God to transform and renew your mind to see others around you the way He sees them. It's never too late to start walking in purity. No matter what you've done or how far you've wondered, Abba is calling you back home. He longs to purify you and love you back to life. He longs to rid you of the past pain and hurt you've experienced.

He loves you infinitely. When you concede to God's ideas on love and purity, you will be able to say to your Boaz someday, "I waited for you and remained pure in my heart, soul, and body to give everything to you." Purity beckons us to deny our flesh and chase after the things of Christ. Purity calls us to be in the world but not of the world. So today, I challenge you dear sister, to remain pure until the day you marry God's best for you.

Daily Prayer

Heavenly Father,

I thank you in advance for all that you are going to do in both my future husband's life and in mine. I pray that you would build us up in purity, keep us both on the narrow road that leads to each other and to you. Help me to walk in purity and to not be led astray by temptation.

I pray that you would mold me into a woman who treats other men as brothers in the faith, not as potential dating partners. I pray that I would not only walk in purity physically, but that my heart and mind would remain pure as well. I pray a covering over my future husband's heart, mind, and body as well in Jesus name. When you bring my Boaz into my life, I pray that we would both walk in love and purity together as a couple and keep us steadfast until our wedding day. I thank you Lord for love, grace, and second chances.

In Jesus name,
Amen

Daily Journal

_____

_____

_____

_____

_____

_____

_____

Scriptures to meditate on:

1 Corinthians 6:13
1 Corinthians 6:18
Hebrew 13:4

Day 26: She Embraces Obedience

Daily Devotion

"So Samuel said: "Has the Lord as great delight in burnt offerings and sacrifices, as in obeying the voice of the Lord? Behold, to obey is better than sacrifice, and to heed than the fat of rams."
1 Samuel 15:22

Samuel realized the importance of obedience to the voice of God. To heed to the Master's voice is better than any work or service you can do. What will you accomplish if you go your own way without asking God what His opinion is on the matter? God's voice should be the first and loudest voice in your life, and His voice should hold the final say.

The instructions God gives us through His word are not to control us or to keep us from living. In fact, they're God's way of protecting us because He loves us so much. He wants us to live the greatest life imaginable, and the guidelines He gives us are not to hurt us, but to keep us on the right track. Obedience will play a vital role in your marriage someday. You must submit yourself to God and your husband, and both of you must submit yourselves and your marriage to Christ daily. Likewise, your husband is called to love you fully and deeply, just as Christ loves the church.

When you submit yourself to God, everything will work together for your good. His ways are above our ways, and when we choose to allow God to write our story, we are abiding by the perfect will of the Father. Today I want to encourage you to fall in love with Christ more and more each day, and allow Him to guide your every step because He has wonderful things in store for you. Stay obedient in this season and watch what God does in your life.

Daily Prayer

Heavenly Father,

I thank you in advance for all that you are going to bring to pass in my life. I pray that you would mold me into a woman who is obedient to your voice. I pray that my actions would line up with your Holy Word, and that I would not be led astray by this world.
   Abba, help me to walk with you every single step of the way. I know that marriage is a calling, and I pray that in everything I do, I would always be obedient to your voice. When you bring my Boaz into my life, I pray that we would both walk in obedience as you lead us into what you have called us to do. I pray that you would shape our marriage into something beautiful as we follow you all the days of our life. Thank you for the work you are doing in my life. I love you, Lord.

In Jesus name,
Amen

Daily Journal

_____

_____

_____

_____

_____

Scriptures to meditate on:

Deuteronomy 11:1
2 Corinthians 10:5
John 14:5

Day 27: She is a Visionary

Daily Devotion

"Where there is no vision, the people perish: but he that keepeth the law, happy is he.
Proverbs 29:18

    This verse tells us that if we do not carry vision with us, we will surely perish. Vision helps us to keep the ultimate goal in mind and pushes us forth into our destiny. Vision is what causes us to set goals for ourselves and strive to become better, therefore it's no secret how essential it is to our growth and success.
    Vision is even important for your mental health, and is a foundational stone for your relationships. Would you marry a man that you couldn't see yourself with in ten or even twenty

years? That is where vision comes in. Vision acts as a safeguard, and helps sustain you and keep your mindset in alignment with the course you are meant to stay on.

God places vision down in our hearts to encourage and strengthen us as we do what He has called us to do. When you find the person God has for you, you will establish a vision together that will carry you through the years. When times get hard in your marriage, come back to the vision God placed in your heart on the day of your wedding to remind you of where you are going. It's essential to become a visionary now and not allow the enemy to rob you of your hope for tomorrow because God has a work to do in your life before and after you meet your Boaz.

Daily Prayer

Heavenly Father,

I thank you for all that you are and all that you are doing in my life. I pray that you would make me into a visionary. Cause me to cling tightly to your promises for my life and not become sidetracked. Whenever I begin to feel as though I am sinking, remind me that you are the anchor that holds me down. Ground me in your holy word.

　　I pray that the vision you have placed in my heart would spring forth in your perfect timing. I pray to always be supportive of my future husband's God-birthed vision. Plant vision in his heart as well as mine. Help us walk the road you have called us to and to carry hope in our hearts every single day. Bring us together in your timing Abba, and help us to always trust in you. I love you, Lord.

*In Jesus name,
Amen*

Daily Journal

Scriptures to meditate on:

Proverbs 3:5-6
Psalm 37:4
Ephesians 5:20

Day 28: She is Resolute

Daily Devotion

"He only is my rock and my salvation, my stronghold; I shall not be greatly shaken."
Psalm 62:2

Insecurity has always been an inward struggle that has not only affect my marriage, but every single aspect of my life. *Am I pretty enough? Will he always love me? Am I too clingy?* For the longest time insecurity kept me back from fully relying on my husband and clinging to him. Even now, I allow insecurity to rob me of my peace, I would be lying if I told you it wasn't still a daily struggle for me. I kept my guard up to my husband for many years, which had the capability of destroying our marriage. I was afraid that if I fully trusted him with everything in me, that I would find myself broken and disappointed someday. Thankfully, God showed me He is my ultimate security, and that I can rest in Him and have no fear. God doesn't give junk to his beloved daughters, and every good and perfect gift comes from Him alone.

When I came to the realization that God loved me and wasn't going to build my heart up only to let me down, I was able to fully grasp onto how much He loves me, and that I didn't need to fear the future. I am totally secure in Jesus, and beloved, so are you. Our worth is in Christ Jesus.

We all have a thorn in the flesh. Maybe for you its lust, addiction, fear, depression, or even anxiety. But you can rest knowing that God is on your side and you will not be shaken. He loves you and has an incredible plan for your life that far outweighs your present circumstance. He is your rock and salvation. He will hold you when you feel like you are falling apart. He is the anchor that will hold you firm when you feel as though you are sinking. And the best part of it all is that you are His daughter and He looks on you with admiration. You have nothing to fear, because God is on your side. You will always rise back up from the ashes because that is exactly how you were your Creator made you, strong and resolute.

Daily Prayer

Heavenly Father,

 In a world that finds security in things that will fail, I pray to always find my security in you alone. You alone are my rock, God. You are mighty to save, and you love me with an everlasting love. I cannot be shaken because you are always by my side.
 I pray that you would mold me into a woman who is stable and resolute, because I know who my Father is. Help me be a rock for my future husband in hard times and help us to always rely on you as our cornerstone so that we will not be shaken, now and when you bring us both together. I pray that we would always run to you and trust in you. I thank you for your love for me. I thank you for molding me into the wife my future husband needs.

*In Jesus name,
Amen*

Daily Journal

_____

_____

_____

_____

_____

_____

_____

Scriptures to meditate on:

Joshua 23:8
Job 11:15

Day 29: She Walks in Confidence

Daily Devotion

"For the LORD will be your confidence and will keep your foot from being caught."
Proverbs 3:26

We spoke on insecurity and stability in Christ yesterday, but today I want to challenge you to dig a little deeper inside of your heart and ask God to bring to the surface anything that isn't a reflection of Him. Insecurity is jealousy's ugly twin sister. If you don't kick insecurity to the curb now, you will find yourself becoming a jealous, miserable person, someone you don't want to be. Sisters, we have to rest in the fact that God will not give us junk. God isn't going to give you a man who will abuse your heart. God made you special and unique, you are unlike any other person on this entire planet.

Psalms 139:14 proclaims that you are "fearfully and wonderfully made," so why hold onto the lies of the enemy any longer, the one who is jealous of you? You were made beautifully, and the creator of the world is mad about you. You hold a special place inside of His heart, His heart skips a beat at the thought of you. Ladies, this is the kind of love that can heal and renew you. If you go into relationship after relationship searching for this kind of love, you will find yourself disappointed and buried deeper within your own insecurities. Let God mend, woo, heal, and renew your heart before you place it in the hands of any other man. You deserve nothing but the best kind of love, and that love starts in the arms of God.

So today my sister, I challenge you to allow God to show you how He sees you. He is so proud of you and wants you to walk in boldness and confidence. Don't allow the enemy to convince you that you are anything less than priceless. You are so special, and you are called to love yourself and see yourself through the eyes of your Father.

Daily Prayer

Heavenly Father,

I thank you for this journey we are walking together. Many days I struggle with being a confident woman. I struggle with feeling as though I am enough and being content in my own skin. But I pray that you begin to mold my heart and mind to see what you see when you look at me.

I pray to become a woman who walks forth boldly in confidence, knowing that I have been blessed and highly favored. I pray that I would not give into the lies of the enemy that I am not good enough. Father, you are where I place my full confidence. Mold me and shape my mind so that I not not carry insecurity into my relationships and future marriage. I thank you for loving, renewing, and healing me.

In Jesus name,
Amen

Daily Journal

_____

_____

_____

_____

_____

_____

_____

Scriptures to meditate on:

1 John 5:14
Ephesians 3:12
Isaiah 32:17

Day 30: She is After God's Own Heart

Daily Devotion

> *"I want to know Christ and the power of His resurrection and the fellowship of His sufferings being conformed to Him in His death,"* Philippians 3:10

Above all, my prayer for you is that you will become a woman after God's own heart, and that you will come to fully know the deepness of the Father's love for you. I pray that you would find yourself in Him, and establish yourself in worship and praise knowing that He is your rock when all around you is sinking sand. God loves you more in a lifetime than a thousand lovers ever could, so I pray that in this season you would find your rest in Him as He molds and prepares you into *the one*. I pray that you would come to know the fullness of God. There is no one and nothing that could ever come close to how much He loves you. I pray that you would embrace this season of singleness as God prepares both you and your future husband. Embrace the journey, and find joy and peace each step of the way. God has wonderful things in store for you and He loves you so very much. God is writing your story, so you have nothing to fear. Just dance with God, and when the time is right, He will let the perfect man cut in.

Daily Prayer

Heavenly Father,

More than anything in this life I long to know you. My heart thirsts for you, my soul aches for your spirit. I pray that I would never be satisfied living a life without you. I pray that you continue to draw me closer each day, and I pray to always put you above all others.

I pray that you would purify my heart, mind, and soul. I want to be more like you. I thank you for what you are doing in my life. I thank you that you have my future husband set aside for me, and I will continue to wait for him until you say the time is right. I pray that we would both chase after you and make it our primary goal to know and pursue you all the days of our life. Thank you for loving me. I love you endlessly, Lord.

In Jesus name,
Amen

Prayer Journal

_____

_____

_____

_____

Scriptures to meditate on:

Deuteronomy 4:29
Matthew 6:33
Hebrews 11:6

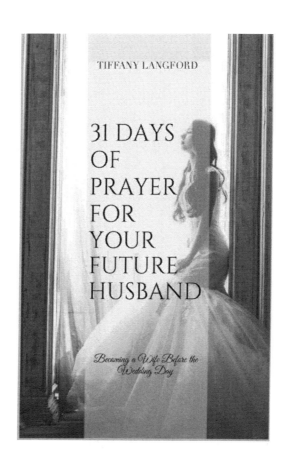

Have you ever wondered why it is important to pray for your future husband? Maybe you have struggled with what words to use and how to pray for the man God has for you. **<u>31 Days of Prayer for Your Future Husband</u>** is a guide to teach you how to pray for the man God has for you and answers a lot of the questions concerning marriage and God's will for your love life that you may have been pondering deep down in your heart.

    This book is designed to help you along your journey as you develop a heart like the biblical character Ruth. It is designed to encourage, guide, and teach you what it means to be a praying wife, long before the wedding day. Through this book you will become more prepared for marriage, and understand the value of what it means to become a praying wife and to pray for your future husband.

    You are made for greatness. God has your love story in His hands. Our culture needs more women who have a heart like Ruth, and I pray this book will be a blessing to you on your journey to wifehood.

To purchase, go to **waitingforyourboaz.com** or grab your copy on **Amazon**!!

About the Author

Tiffany Langford is an influential American author, blogger, and advocate of love.

She is the founder of the web-based ministry Waiting for Your Boaz, where she serves a community of nearly one million women through avenues such as her blog, social media, and <u>daily devotionals.</u> Her mission is to spread the love and gospel of Jesus and encourage women both single and married with God's ideas on love, marriage, courtship, and relationships. In just five years, Waiting for your Boaz has blossomed into an influential website and continues to grow leaps and bounds by showing the love of God to a hurting world.

Tiffany, a Southeastern Kentucky native, now resides in Myrtle Beach, SC with her husband and daughter.

Connect with Tiffany at **waitingforyourboaz.com** and on all social media outlets.

Made in the USA
Columbia, SC
16 August 2021